Agnes Török is a Swedish spc
performing in English and Swe
awards, been featured at inter
performed on four continents.

CH00393503

Török regularly collaborates w.... ... ___, ...
workshops for young people and adults, and releases crowd
funded poetry videos online.

She became a spoken word poet (in her second language) after
a physical disability shut down her ability to write or type and
she had to learn to write by speech. This is her debut published
collection.

Her story is one of resilience. So is the story of this book.

HAPPINESS IS AN ART FORM

AGNES TÖRÖK

Burning Eye

BurningEyeBooks
Never Knowingly
Mainstream

This edition published by Burning Eye Books 2016

www.burningeye.co.uk
@burningeyebooks

Burning Eye Books
15 West Hill, Portishead, BS20 6LG

ISBN 978-1-909136-86-1

HAPPINESS IS AN ART FORM

CONTENTS

HAPPINESS IS PERSONAL 11
WHO HERE 13
SIX THINGS YOU DIDN'T KNOW ABOUT ME 16
EARTHQUAKE LIVING 20
THIS IS THE POEM THAT MAKES YOU SMILE 25

HAPPINESS IS SOCIAL 31
(MY DAD) THE CYCLIST 33
STRUGGLE SONGS 36
HAPPIEST WHEN I'M DRINKING 38
'BEING UNHAPPY IS SELFISH' 39
LIFE OR DEATH BILINGUALISM 43
INOSCULATION 46
THE OLD LADIES IN THE HOSPITAL 48

HAPPINESS IS POLITICAL 53
HAPPINESS IS USELESS 55
WORK ISN'T WORKING 57
I AM THE BEST 61
WORTHLESS 63

COLLECTIVE HAPPINESS IS POLITICAL 69
TEACH ME 71
THE FUCK OFF ACCOUNT 74
FRIENDS WITH THE RACISTS 77

INDIVIDUAL HAPPINESS IS POLITICAL 83
I COULDN'T BE HAPPIER 85
THIS IS MY BODY 86
COCA-COLA HAPPINESS 88
WHEN DID YOU REALISE 90
THIS LITTLE FIGHT OF MINE 92
THIS IS A GOOD TIME 94

HAPPINESS IS AN ART FORM   99
  YOU SAY 'POETRY'   101
  THE HEART IS A MUSCLE   102

FEEDING HAPPINESS   107
WRITING EXERCISES:
  MIND BLOB   110
  REMEMBERING THE GOOD STUFF   114
  RECIPE FOR SELF-CARE   118
  WHAT IS IN OUR POWER   122
  RETELLING THE STORY   125
  LETTER TO A STRANGER   126
  TIMELINE OF LEARNING   129
  QUESTIONS AND ANSWERS   132
  LETTER TO A FRIEND   135

HAPPINESS MANIFESTO   143
  ART FOR ART'S SAKE   144

HAPPINESS IS PERSONAL

I spent all of 2015 living according to current happiness research.

During the year, I tried to adjust my habits according to facts and figures, in a strange and scientific pursuit of a happier life. I battled with challenges. I celebrated victories. And I used the research to guide me through both. In the process, I learnt a few things I think you might want to know too. A few things that, probably, deep inside yourself, you already know.

For example, I learnt that happiness and unhappiness aren't polar opposites. Rather, they are simultaneous experiences. On any given day, any given one of us will have things that are working in our lives, things we appreciate and are grateful for – perhaps it's our friends, our families, or our good memories – but we will also have things that worry us, frustrate us, and challenge us severely.

Mental health, wellbeing, happiness – call it what you like. It is part of what it is to be human. Part of what we all struggle with – in different ways, to different extents, at different times. The research shows that there are aspects of this human happiness that we can impact and change in various ways. And the research might just help.

These poems are about what I learnt during that year of living according to happiness research. About struggling, about overcoming, and about learning. About learning slowly, to appreciate the good stuff more – to take less of the good in my life for granted. About learning to not face the difficult stuff alone – about asking for help and recognising that happiness is bigger than any one of us. It is us together.

who here has ever felt
happy?
who here has ever felt like
they're not appreciating the
good things
enough?
who here has ever felt
overwhelmed
by the bad things?
who here has ever felt
even for a moment
like the bad things
might
outweigh
the good?
who here has not known
how to change things?

I don't think it's just me

who here
when they think about the word
HAPPY
pictures
a bunch of people
in pastel-coloured shirts
laughing together
in a perfectly clean kitchen?
who here
when they think about the word
HAPPY
pictures someone
skydiving?
who here
when they think about the word
HAPPY
pictures a bunch of people
jumping
at the exact same time

on a beach
in a sunset?
who here pictures
a beautiful slim white woman
laughing alone with a salad?

I know I do

who here
when they think about the word
HAPPY
pictures someone
thinner
than them?
or younger
than them?
or healthier
than them?
or richer
than them?

who here
when they think about the word
HAPPY
pictures themselves?

I never used to

who here has ever made a
New Year's resolution
to become thinner
healthier
or
save more money?
who here has ever made a promise
to themselves
to figure out what makes them happy
and how they can do more of it?

I am only just now learning how

I am twenty-three years old
when for the first time in my life
I decide to spend a year figuring out
what makes me happy
and how I can do more of it
and I am only just now
learning how
to be happy

I have spent the majority of my life
memorising useless facts
to regurgitate them
on command
at tests
and then promptly
forget all about them

yet I am only just now
learning how
to be happy

you'd have thought
this was an earlier
priority

but I am only just now
learning how
to be happy

and in the end
I think this is stuff no one can teach you
we're going to have to teach ourselves

because I am only just now
learning how
to be happy

and I hope
you've started learning
too

ONE
my name is Agnes Török
the reason you can't pronounce my last name
is because it's not a real last name
it's fake
it's made up
I'm serious
I didn't make it up though
it was my great-grandfather who invented it
but it was for a good reason
I'm from Sweden
but my great-grandfather grew up in Hungary
as Jewish intellectuals in Hungary
my family knew that it would not be long until they were
deported to concentration camps

(this is probably not how you expected
a book about happiness
to start – sorry!
I promise
we'll get there!)

for my great-grandfather's family
things didn't look good
so they exchanged their Jewish last name for a new one
one that would explain their dark hair
their dark eyes
their facial features
Török
the Hungarian word for 'Turkish'
literally
the Hungarian word for Turkish
that is how stupid the officials were
that if you changed your last name
to the Hungarian word for Turkish
and had a whole lotta luck
there was a chance the officials would go
Jewish
Jewish

Jewish
oh – no, they're Turkish, they're fine
and you would not be sent to concentration camp

because of the idiocy of officials
and a whole lotta luck
my great-grandfather's family survived
and my grandfather fled to Sweden
where he met a Swedish woman
and they had children
and their oldest child grew up
and had a child
that child is me
if it wasn't for this unpronounceable lie of a last name
I probably would never have been born
and would never be sat here
writing to you
about happiness

TWO
I have the world's worst sense of direction
honestly
I have gotten lost on my own street
more than once
(it's a very short street)

THREE
I have lived in three countries
and written in two languages
this is not my first
but it is the first where I don't mind feeling lost

FOUR
I didn't write this book
because I know everything there is to know
about happiness
(I definitely don't)
I wrote this because
when it comes to happiness
I am still pretty lost
but there are things that have helped
things like learning more about the science

like understanding the facts and figures
like writing about it all
that have helped me
I thought sharing
what I'd learned
with you
might
in some
small
way
help you too

FIVE
there are experiences of feeling good and feeling bad
of joys and challenges
that I have lived
and I will tell you about
like having to cope with serious illness
and living with mental ill-health
like overcoming physical disability
     like the joy of eating chocolate cake
     and the importance of daring to ask for help
but there are also experiences of feeling good and feeling bad
that I haven't lived
and I won't pretend I have
I have never been diagnosed with depression
I have never found solace in praying
I have never tried to run a marathon
you might have
you might know all about that
     (and I would love to hear your story)

all of our journeys are different
I can only speak for mine
but I invite you to take the time while you read
to think about your journey
your life
your good times and your bad
your joys and your challenges
I hope having this time to think and feel and reflect
might help you find some answers in yourself
whether that is to focus on the good things

or fight on through the bad things
or to recognise that sometimes the strongest thing
       is to ask for help
I think
this
this right here
right now
this might just be the right time
to start thinking about you

SIX
I think reading is an act of compassion
by choosing to read about someone else
we decide to care about a perfect stranger
thank you for being compassionate

sometimes
at the end of a poem
the person who reads the poem
responds with their face
it makes me feel good when people do
it makes me feel happy
for example
sometimes
at the end of a poem
the person who reads the poem
smiles
for example
sometimes
at the end of a poem
the person who reads the poem
smiles and turns the page with care
for example
you could try it
right now

EARTHQUAKE LIVING

living with mental ill-health
is knowing that you are living in an earthquake zone
that anxiety builds over time
inside you
like friction
parts of who you are
pushing against each other
until one day
one hour
one minute
every once in a while
you feel the earth shaking beneath your feat
you feel yourself slipping and crashing at once

living with mental ill-health
is knowing that your body is an earthquake zone
your mind is an earthquake zone
and there is no leaving it
there is no moving away
no going on holiday
there is only learning to notice the preshakes
learning to read the signals
before disaster strikes
– worry, numbness, pressure on chest, rainclouds in mind –
      friction

when the best you can do
to protect yourself
from the quakes
is to read the signals
      you become an expert at resilience

slowly
you will learn the difference in the anxiety attack scale
beginning at
1 – small
take a deep breath
focus
count anything available to you

put hand on stomach
notice your own breathing
you are here
2 - sizeable
find a bathroom to cry in, find a friend to call
it will all be over soon
3, 4 – rough
find a room to lock yourself in
shut off the lights
unplug the sockets
lie down and wait for the quakes to subside
the crying to end
the shaking to stop
5, 6 – you'll want to find a good archway
you know the walls will come tumbling down
maybe the whole building this time
the roof with it
you will remember what you wish you did not
imagine what you wish you could not
you will feel every emotion at once
and every fear will for a moment seem absolutely real
all at once
for a moment you will be convinced you did not get out alive
you only imagined it
and the walls
will
tumble

those days
those days find somewhere safe
someone safe
and stay put until the walls have fallen
until the windows have shattered
and you are ready to go out into the morning light
of a new day
and rebuild again

7, 8, 9 – sometimes whole villages are subsumed
in the quakes
house after house comes crashing down
your past
your future

the now is consumed
is there anything
anything good in the world?

10 – when the worst days come
you will learn to build yourself bunkers
and wait it out
you will learn to repeat to yourself
through the shaking
the crying
the numbness and the overwhelmingness
you will learn to speak to yourself in the calmest way
you know how
repeating
this too shall pass
this too shall pass
this
too
shall
pass

and the words will become hollow for a while
until you remember again
until you remember that there is a time after earthquakes
that you have lived through this before
that you will live through it again
that there is always an after
always a new beginning

living with mental ill-health
is living in an earthquake zone
is knowing that you must build your foundations strong
or they will come crashing down
when the next disaster strikes
when the next tremors come from nowhere

living with mental ill-health
is learning how to rebuild
again and again and again
every time the walls come crushing down
every time a whole village
so carefully built
crashes into nothingness

learning to rebuild
yourself and your life
again and again
stronger each time
surer each time
you are
learning the meaning of resilient

resilient
does not mean strong
it means able to build strength
time and time again

resilient
does not mean stability
it means the ability to come crashing down
and stand back up again

living with mental ill-health
is living in an earthquake zone
only the zone is your body
the fracture is your memory
the friction is your sense of self

rebuilding the houses is learning to
love yourself again
trust yourself again
believe yourself again
rebuilding the village
is slowly
slowly
learning to trust others too

living with mental ill-health
is knowing
there will always be another quake
it may be smaller
and you may be better prepared
you may identify the signs more easily with time
– isolation, exhaustion, numbness –
but you cannot control the earthquakes
you did not cause the slippage

cannot undo the friction
can only wait for what is coming
and patiently
slowly
rebuild

and that is true resilience
this earthquake living
of ours

this is the poem that makes you smile
you don't know it yet
but I promise
it does

because this poem smells
like a hug from your mother
the cool side of your pillow in the morning
like the air of somewhere new
somewhere you've never been before
but always dreamed of going

this poem sounds like one of your granddad's jokes
and the way he'd laugh
before he even got to the punchline
you know the one

this poem sounds like
the opening of an acceptance letter
the love of your life
saying YES
this poem sounds like the first song you ever
really
loved

and it feels like the dance you used to do
when you listened to it
this poem feels like the fact that
you probably still know how to do that dance
and maybe practise it sometimes
          when no one's watching
this poem feels like
the first time anyone ever told you they loved you
          do you remember it?

this poem tastes like your favourite candy
like reaching out your tongue and tasting the snow
this poem tastes like hope
like the first swear word you ever learned

and the first time you used it
in front of your parents

this poem looks like
the drawings you made of your sister
when you were four
and you drew her face
like a monster's
because
she was being mean
and it would take a full
five minutes
until you made up
and forgot all about it

this is the poem that makes you smile
because
you
fill it
with everything that does

this poem is the adorable Google image searches
you pretend you don't do
this poem
is the bathing of kittens
the yawning of dogs
the jam-smeared faces of babies

this poem sounds like
your best friend's laughter
like someone new saying
'I trust you'
like coming home

and it looks like the dreams you unpacked
in the first flat you ever lived in on your own

this poem feels like jumping in puddles
at the age of five
just 'cause you can
just 'cause you don't have to be grown-up yet

this poem tastes like
eating ice-cream for breakfast
because now that
you *are* a grown-up
          no one can really tell you not to

this poem is the nights you go to sleep
laughing
and the mornings you wake up
still drunk
on life

this poem feels like
how you can turn
a shit day
around
by reading
this poem

HAPPINESS IS SOCIAL

One of the first things I learnt about happiness is that none of us are happy on our own.

We need other people for our happiness just like they need us. And us taking care of ourselves – our physical health and mental health – benefits more than us. It makes us more able to take care of the people around us – our social relationships, our communities and our societies.

For example, when researchers collated data based on self-reported happiness surveys (essentially asking people the question 'How happy are you today?'), they found some interesting results. It turns out that people who consider themselves relatively happy are also likely to be friendlier, more generous and more interested in other people than those people who consider themselves to be relatively unhappy.

I think that is wrong. By which I mean, I think it's the other way around. I think that when we are friendlier, more generous and more interested in other people, we become happier. Which would make sense. Because the more we care for the people around us, the more likely we are to be able to ask for help when we need it, and to feel that we are not alone in our most difficult times.

Statistically speaking, women often feel guilty about doing things we know make us happier – taking more time for ourselves, or doing less housework, or starting a new hobby. And women, much more often than men, often feel that it would be selfish to change their lives in ways that would make them happier. That taking more time for themselves, or the things they enjoy, would mean giving up their duties to others.

So I will say it here, in case no one has told you before.

You deserve to be happy.

And by a strange coincidence, you doing what makes you happy actually helps the people around you too!

Because happiness is social.

that time my dad nearly died
I learnt
something important
I learnt
that I'm a
bitch
to people who nearly die

he tore his hamstring
and broke his neck
trying to break some
cycling record
and it nearly broke me
yet when I saw him in the hospital
he just smiled
said how happy he was to be alive
and just to see me again

– maybe it was the morphine –

but maybe
it was because he's a cyclist
        he plans for aching muscles
        loves a long road ahead
        and believes in the power of
                the journey

– then again
it was probably the morphine –

but he just smiled
said he was so grateful
things hadn't gone worse

he said this, mind
wearing a neck brace
his face covered in multicoloured bruises
still uncertain of whether he'd walk again

but he looked
so
happy

I didn't feel the same

he may be the long-distance triathlete
but I've lived
far too far
from him
for far too long
to ignore
what distance
feels like

so instead of listening to his stories
of realisations
and the learning curve
how hard times
teach us how loved we really are
instead of calm and quiet
and contemplation over the road travelled

instead of
'I'm here'
and
'everything will be OK'

instead
I climbed up next to him in his hospital bed
put my heavy head
on his struggling lungs
and told him that if he
ever
ever
died
I would kill him

if he didn't wear a helmet
or he pushed himself too far
or if he got too old or too sick
that was not a good enough excuse

my dad was back on his bike within months

but he promised me
he promised
he's never falling off again
without letting me catch him

STRUGGLE SONGS

I grew up
to the sound of
struggle songs
I never knew my country's
national anthem
I learnt the
socialist international
and there was only one year
in my mother's history book
the year of female suffrage

1919
Stockholm, Sweden
they signed the bill
and, Mummy, I remember still
don't know how I could ever forget

you see
I never came out to you
there was never a closet to hide in
because you told me
you told me you didn't care who I loved
as long as I never hated
that I could be anything
anything I wanted
(except a racist)
that you would always respect my opinions
(so long as I was a feminist)
        and Mum – it's funny

how you've struggled so silently
under others' banners

because I remember the protests, Mamma
I remember the demonstrations
and how the one thing
that could make you really angry
        was injustice

but I never remember you crying
and I imagine you must have cried

see, I remember days you couldn't get out of bed
when the hatred of one individual
killed the voice of a nation
by stabbing her
three times in the gut
I remember you'd seen her earlier that day
that it was you and her against the world
that she always wore red
and I remember
that you fell in love
when he took care of you
after the prime minister
and your party fell
to the sound
of a bullet

but I never remember you crying

and Mother
I would like to hear your cries now
not because you still carry them inside
but because I never got to help you with the burden

you see, I grew up to the sound of struggle songs
and I've not stopped singing them
will never stop singing them
because
a luta continua
sikhula sonke
and
upp till kamp emot kvalen

I grew up to the sound of struggle songs
and you
you
were my melody

HAPPIEST WHEN I'M DRINKING

how come I'm always happiest
when I'm drinking
tea
happier by candlelight
than in front of the TV?

how come I'm always happiest
when I'm not alone
happier surrounded by friends and family
love and laughter
than I am on my own?

how come I'm always happiest
doing the simple things
happier eating, drinking, talking
with good company
than doing anything more money could buy me?

'being unhappy is selfish'
she says
and to me that sounds extreme
I mean, I don't want to place guilt or responsibility
where you have too much
your mental ill-health or mental illness is never your fault
will never be your fault
I'm just trying to tell you
that you are also caring for others
      by caring for yourself
      that it is not selfish to practice self-care

statistically speaking
there is nothing you can do
that will benefit the people around you more
than you making sure
you are doing what is in your power
to be well
to appreciate the good stuff
to build resilience in the face of the difficulties
to ask for the help you need
personal or professional
to be well

one of the most generous things you can do
is to do what you can
to be happy

I said happy, OK?
not some always-smiling
never-complaining
impeccable dressed
eternally self-sacrificing
1950s housewife
      version of yourself

I said happy
not more positive
or more enthusiastic
or better at making packed lunches

I said happy
not more of a
physical embodiment
of a motivational poster

I said happy

happy like taking time for yourself every day
like sleeping and eating
and moving
like talking about what's going on
like asking for help

you don't need to justify
taking time to
take care of your *basic health*
you don't need an excuse
for your right
to feel good

I said happy
happy
like being messy and sloppy with laughter
happy
like sharing the difficult stuff with people you trust
happy
like doing the things you love without excuses
without justification
happy
like painting your toenails in glittery disco colours in the
middle of
the winter
even though you don't have time
even though no one is going to see it
even though it doesn't make sense
just because it make you *smile*
when you get out of bed in the morning
and that is worth having toes that look ridiculous

because as it turns out
not doing the things that make you happy
not taking time for your physical health and your mental health

doesn't help
it doesn't help us
and it doesn't help others
as much as we tend to think

it has been scientifically proven
that happy people are
more altruistic
more helpful more productive more creative more resilient
more interested in others
than other people

It doesn't stop there
as it turns out
happy people
make better friends colleagues citizens partners and parents

this is not to tell you to feel bad
about struggling
about having a hard time getting out of bed in the morning
about having shit days
     everyone does
         happy people too

this is not to tell you
you can't be annoyed or tired or stressed or angry or ill
     everyone is
         happy people too

this is not to place blame for your struggles

this is just to tell you that you have the right
nay, the licence
to *take care of yourself*
that there is nothing wrong with taking time
to make sure that you're OK
if you are going to continue to be able
to take care of others
you need to start by taking care
of yourself

so take care of your happiness

it is fragile
it depends on you caring for it
catering to it
prioritising it
every day
even when it doesn't seem rational
even when you don't feel you have time
even when you don't feel you have energy

and asking others to help when you don't feel able to do it all
there is no shame in that

when you do
when you take care of yourself and your health and your
happiness
when you let others help and take care of you
when you prioritise the things that make you feel good
you are doing the most selfless thing
you are giving other people the right to do the same

a recent study at the University of Edinburgh
conducted by a team of researchers led by Dr Thomas Bak
based on data from the Lothian Birth Cohort
found that
learning a second language
slows down the ageing of the brain
decreases the effects of Alzheimer's

and I have come to terms
with losing mobility of limbs
and functions of several
      vital organs
but take away my mind
and I am hemlös i mig själv
sorry – I mean
take away my mind
and I am homeless
in my own skin

because I can't bear to part
with my mind or my memories
I bring you
life or death
bilingualism

because I need to sing these languages
like mitt hjärta slår i otakt
because my heartbeat tries to catch up on itself
varje gång jag reprogram my brain's language selection
because denna schizofreni
får inte plats i ett enskilts språks poesi
because language learning eradicates the borders between
you and me
I bring you
life or death
bilingualism

a recent study at the University of Edinburgh
conducted by a team of researchers led by Dr Thomas Bak

based on data from the Lothian Birth Cohort
failed to find
that languages are wings
the more you speak
the higher you fly
the more you see

like
have you ever
andats
a love
or fingertoppssmekt
a loneliness?

then what do you know about love?
what do you know about loneliness?

because I've had to know
I bring you
life or death
bilingualism

because
a recent study at the University of Edinburgh
conducted by a team of researchers led by Dr Thomas Bak
based on data from the Lothian Birth Cohort
failed to find

that bilingualism is a butcher's knife
it splits your very being into separate compartments
labels them in letters the others don't understand
before it forces you to expand
beyond who you were
in every direction
until your insides have become so wide
that no lover or friend
can ever fill all the voids you've created inside
because they will never know
all the conjugations of you

remember what I told you about loneliness?

on the other hand
is there anything more beautiful
than our ability to speak across boundaries
boundaries like
nations
and borders
and tongues
boundaries like
flesh
and bone
and blood
to speak *straight into hearts* and be heard?

a recent study at the University of Edinburgh
conducted by a team of researchers...

you know what?
fuck it
a recent study
was conducted in only one language
so *screw the study*

INOSCULATION

inosculation is the process by which several trees grow into
each other
and become one

the branches of two trees first grow separately
in proximity to each other
until they touch
this process can take years

at this point
the bark on the touching surfaces is gradually worn away
as the trees move in the wind

when they have become skinless
the raw wood begins growing together
making one giant tree

the reason I am telling you this
is I have never had just one family tree
I grew up part of a forest

my family have known inosculation better than anyone
as much a practice of personal politics
as collective solidarity
nearly every member of my extended family
has at some point
departed from their previous relationship
and set off branches in new directions
while never letting go of the old

finding ways to see the sunshine after
separation, divorce, heartbreak
moving
to share branches on which children can grow up
as part of trees of wildly different fruits and flowers
finding ways to blossom
again and again
staying friends and
caring for the roots they'd grown away from
creating new green shoots every new spring

my family were not so much nuclear
as unclear
branches stretched in every direction
on our conglomeration of blood, and love, and friendship
I grew up with the knowledge that family
is the family you choose
that as long as you practise honesty and compassion
they will always choose you too

I grew up blessed with strong roots stretching across countries
and languages
and wide branches to keep me safe at night
a blanket of leaves over my head
just sparse enough I could always see the stars
just thick enough
I always knew I was enveloped by love

as I grew tall enough to reach the highest shoots
I departed
climbed onto a seed
and flew south with the wind

I knew I'd find just as many people to grow part of there

it started small
host families in France
newfound sisters in Turkey, nephews in Zambia
mothers in India, brothers in Nepal
a whole extended family in South Africa
and then
then there was Scotland
sometimes I had to leave before our roots had grown deep
enough
and it hurt to stretch our branches across the oceans
but family was always the family we chose

I have stepped off that seed now
started growing roots deep enough to maintain my stability
while integrating into other trees

I hope to one day build a new forest

inosculation is the process
by which several trees grow into each other
and become one

THE OLD LADIES IN THE HOSPITAL

the old ladies in the hospital have got it all figured out
they talk about everything
crown you family
when you were stranger only a minute ago
they talk about the good things
like how nice the nurses are for bringing extra toast at night
and whose grandchild is meant to come for visiting hour today
they joke about everything
'why, I don't know what I ever did to that man Parkinson for
him to give me his disease'

nothing is serious enough to take serious
when death may be at the door
these beds have been rolled around
more than once before
I don't know who left
or through what door
for me to earn a place
but I know I no longer need to earn it

because the old ladies in the hospital
have got it all figured out
when things get tough
you talk about the worries
and the scaries
and you get through them
one smile
one compliment
– and yeah –
one cup of tea
at a time

ain't no
each man for himself
here
ain't no
survival of the fittest
here
it's the survival of those

most able to cooperate
the survival of those
most able to care
for more than themselves
it's the survival of us
collectively

what does it matter if I get better
if you get worse?
how could I be winning
if we are losing?
so it is with society
and so it is with ward 210

because the old ladies in the hospital
have got it all
figured out
when things get real rough
I mean when things get *real rough*
when Jessie
struggles to reach her straw
only to get it stuck
so far down her throat
that she starts suffocating
and Nancy
is too far away from her walker
to reach her on time
when the rest of us
have too many things
plugged into our bloodstreams
to move
when things get real rough
you call for Help
capital H
but when Help's come
and Help's Helped
you ask how Help's doing today
because no one's life is easy
did Help get some rest after her shift last night?
has her youngest stopped crying from the toothache?
you listen to Help too
because we are all in this together

the old ladies in the hospital have got it all figured out
because they are fearless in the face of fear
because they will literally
hang their old laundry out in public
and flash each other by opening their gowns
– daily –
before they will feel shameful in the face of shame

because they put their scars
and hearts
and minds
out in the open
you know you can trust them
        with your life

HAPPINESS IS POLITICAL

What would happen if we took happiness seriously?

One of my favourite facts about happiness is that, statistically speaking, if you were to ask any person – on any street corner of any city, of any village, in any country on any continent on this planet – if you were to ask them 'What do you want for your children?' (or your hypothetical future children) nearly every single one would tell you, 'I just want them to be happy.'

I think that's kind of amazing. I think that with all the perceived differences between us in values or priorities, it is amazing that here is one of extremely few things that, statistically, unite us all.

What would happen if we took that seriously? What would happen if we took seriously the fact that what we, as a species, want for the next generation is for them to have what they need to 'just be happy'?

Well, as it turns out, if we took happiness seriously, that would have some profoundly political implications. For example, we would need to acknowledge that certain economic and political structures, like poverty and austerity, make huge parts of the human population much less happy than they otherwise would be. That structural inequalities like racism, sexism and homophobia measurably decrease people's wellbeing.

For example, we would have to try to imagine and build societies that are more about community, and less about corporations – more about people, and less about profit. What would it look like if we tried?

What would happen if we took happiness seriously?

'happiness is useless'
it doesn't do anything
doesn't produce anything
doesn't consume anything
by any account of how we evaluate our lives
and our societies
happiness is useless
it doesn't show up on any of our measurements
– and yet it is one of few things
worth trying to measure

'happiness is useless'
it doesn't achieve anything
doesn't succeed at anything
there are no medals for it
no honorary speakers
no lifetime awards
– and yet it is one of few things
worth striving for

'happiness is useless'
it will not improve your national economy
will not shrink the deficit
cannot save you from climate change
will not protect you from the war
happiness is useless
– and yet it is one of few priorities
that we all agree on

'happiness is useless'
– and yet it makes all the difference in the world
when we have it
everything in our lives is coloured by it
when we lose it
or we struggle to find it
or we wonder if we ever had it at all
everything in our lives
speaks of its absence

'happiness is useless'
we can't put a price tag on it
can't instrumentalise it
can't sell it
can't corrupt it
can't manipulate it
can't use it for our own purposes

happiness is useless
we can't use it for anything
– *except to create*
more
happiness

happiness is useless
– *and that is exactly*
why we need it
so much

We work too much. Too little.
Earn too much. Too little.
Consume too much. Too little.
In an increasingly unequal world
work isn't working.

for the absolute majority of people on this planet
work isn't working
there isn't enough of it to go around
and when there is the pay is bad
the conditions are worse
and work eats away at people without paying them enough to
eat
to let their kids go to sleep with full bellies
and without nightmares of debt and homelessness

work isn't working
doesn't create enough pay or security
to not constantly worry about the next rent instalment
next broken boiler or ripped school uniform
too often
work isn't working
and the majority
become isolated, disheartened, exhausted or resigned
forced to cope with worry and stress that tears away at you
creating illness and mental ill-health

in a system of extreme scarcity and excessive abundance
in a system of unparalleled inequality
work isn't working

too many work too much
work themselves into stress-related illness
ulcers, heart attacks, injuries
create lives so focused around work
we struggle to manage daily tasks
of cooking, cleaning, eating, sleeping
work so much our relationships lose out
so much we become ever more isolated

so much our only reassurance becomes success
the validation of
income figures or Facebook likes
– I have been there so many times
statistically speaking
you probably have too

thinking happiness is just around the corner
at the next achievement
next pay cheque
next holiday
and it's not

in an increasingly unequal world
work isn't working
for anyone
isn't creating the things that make us
happy

the problem is
we have a whole economy
structured around work
but work on its own has no value
work needs to produce something for the people who do the work
and the societies in which that work is done
or else work has no value
no meaning
no point
there is a disconnect between what we assume the economy does
and what the economy actually does
because work isn't working

I wonder what a happy economy would look like

it might look like this:
those able to work working
with something that mattered to them
and everyone working less
our planet would have time to breathe
our healthcare systems would sigh relief at no longer having to
deal with all the heart and coronary disease
that are caused by the pressure of the 9–5 becoming the 7–11

becoming the around-the-clock
the societal standstill caused by the worry of knowing that you
cannot take risks
because if you fail there is no safety net to catch you
no support system to keep you on your feet
that worry would be gone
in its place
a security that could bring out creativity
could allow for full potentials to be realised and fulfilled

imagine this
having an economy that was structured around care
around concern and focus on the wellbeing
of the world's inhabitants
everyone doing something meaningful
everyone working less
we'd have parents who had time to spend with their kids
partners who had time to appreciate each other
friends who had time to talk
communities who'd have time to become and to be
people who had time to find their purpose and their creativity
not always chasing the next pay cheque

every piece of evidence indicates that
this is what we need
that the economists don't know what's good for us
that the politicians know even less
that working like this, buying like this
not having time for our relationships, our communities like this
not being able to use our full potential and creativity for fear of
poverty and homelessness
this
is killing us

what research shows makes humans happy is
community, appreciation of what we have, time to explore our
own interests
creating art, feeling useful, being part of something bigger than
ourselves

not working for money to buy things to have the energy
to go back to working for money

and yet it's what we've built our entire economies on
assuming that having more stuff will make us happier
when every study shows that
once we have the basics
we need time and people more than we need cash and bling

just one little thing could solve it all
imagine this:
work isn't working
but it could

I AM THE BEST
or 'On Naming Your Empire Great (Britain)'

I'm great
I know I must be great
because I said I was
and I'm great

I'm the best
I know I must be the best
because I said I was
and I'm great

I'm developed
I know I must be developed
because I said I was
and I'm great

and I'm great
and I'm developed
and you're not

you're not developed
because you don't have reality TV
or fast food
or landfills
and they're great
I know they must be great
because I have them
and I'm great

and you're not great
and you're not developed
because your people only have what they need
instead of every product they've ever been told
they should want
and you're not developed
because your people grow their own food
instead of buying it
pre-packaged from supermarkets
and you're not developed

because your people have
community
instead of
Facebook friends
and that's not great

that's not great because
I'm not like that
and I'm great
I'm great
and I don't have any of that
I don't have that
because I gave it up years ago
I developed past it
or I lost it
or I'm not sure
but I'm sure it's not great
because I'm great
and I'm not like that

I'm great
I'm great and you're not because you're different
I'm the best
I'm the best and you're not because you're different
I'm developed
I'm developed and you're not because you're weird

so you can be
underdeveloped
and I'll be
developed
and you should listen to me
for how to develop right

because I'm great
because I'm great and I know I must be great
because someone great said I was
it
was
me

give me a student
any student
give me only one definition of success
and only one way to
make it
give me academic excellence
give me full-time extracurriculars
give me part-time job to
pay the bills
give me internship
followed by internship
followed by internship
followed by
       internship?

give me a lifetime of debt
then tell me I am worthless
tell me my labour is not worth
paying
for
tell me it's a favour to hire me
      for free

go on
tell me I am worthless

when in this country
millions of people
compete for thousands of jobs
call it their own personal failure
when they don't all get one
when the young
and the old
and the sick
have no way into a labour market
ever contracting
ever decreasing
when you take money
out of their opportunities for education and health

call it their fault
call them lazy
call them benefit scroungers
call it a
'culture of dependency'

go on
tell us we are worthless

say it's not political
say it's
'just the way it is'
that food banks can be cut
but big banks need be bailed out
that the minimum wage can stagnate
and benefits be chucked off entirely
but when the 1% made more
off the first year of the financial crisis
than they had for the thirty years before

      call it *austerity*

go on
tell us we are worthless

rebrand public failure into personal competition
rebrand it filling your CV
rebrand it increasing your skill sets
rebrand it exposure and networking
as we volunteer and intern
volunteer and intern
digging ourselves ever deeper into debt
ever deeper into despair

go on
tell us we are worthless

tell me unemployment levels skyrocketing
has nothing to do with it
tell me being more likely to end up on the street
than in a graduate job
has nothing to do with it

go on
tell me we're all middle class now

call call centre workers and shelf stackers
garbage handlers and cleaners
call one out of five working for less
than the minimum wage
which is less than the living wage
          'just middle class in the making'

go on
tell us we are worthless

occupy my body
as if it were some resource you could use
to raise the GDP
broken back from all the heavy lifting
crumbling knees from all those hours standing
depression and stress from the worry

how will I pay the rent this month
how will she support the kids
how will he pay the medical bills

go on
tell us we are worthless
tell us the only thing
not working
about this system
          is us

COLLECTIVE HAPPINESS IS POLITICAL

Or, caring for more than ourselves can be a radical act.

In my year of living according to happiness research, I also read a lot of self-help books. And no matter how great, how kind, how thought-through, they tended to have one problem in common: they tended to talk about happiness as a wholly individual thing. But the research shows us, time and time again, that it's not.

Because happiness is social. Because the societies we live in, the world we live in, impact on our mental health. Because the communities we are part of, the relationships we rely on, are the greatest resource for our wellbeing.

In fact, one of the top tips given by current UK happiness researchers is to 'be part of something greater than yourself'. We need purpose beyond ourselves, projects and aims and missions that are bigger than us – to feel that our lives are meaningful. To feel that our struggles are important and worth fighting. To feel happy.

For me, being part of 'something greater than myself' has been organising for social justice. For me, it's been recognising that other people's wellbeing, even that of perfect strangers, even half the world away, matters for my wellbeing. Matters to me. That I cannot be perfectly happy while others suffer. But that it adds to my happiness to try to help, in any small way I can, to make the world a slightly better place.

And that starts with caring for more than ourselves.

TEACH ME

teach me how to be an ally
to your struggle
teach me how to be strong
for the both of us
when I am beat
when I am beat down
and bloodied
when newspaper articles and election results
have pushed my heart deep underground
frozen for winter
not to thaw
until a new kind of Arab Spring
springs
from all that is broken about this world

when I feel hopeless and lost
when I give in and give up
hand me something to fight with
that doesn't involve throwing rocks
give me something to fight for
that doesn't include
hating those who fight against

don't let me be a
them
to your battle

instead
sit me down
tell me your stories
sing me your struggle songs
and I will do the same for you

teach me how to be an ally
to your struggle

in a world of political promises
as hollow as bones
it is easy to train fists before training arguments

in a world of paper manifestos
it is not hard to burn too bright
for due process
in a system this flammable
it is not strange
that some of us would rather start the fire
than build futures
if we still have to
watch
them
burn

so teach me how to be an ally to your struggle
I'm a good listener
I make decent coffee for political meetings
and I can hold hands
as well as I can hold placards
so sit down next to me
and let's talk

let's talk
like it matters
because it does
because it's one of few things
that always do

count
this
figuring-out-how-to-live-together thing
this
figuring-out-how-to-live-with-ourselves thing

teach me how to be an ally to your struggle
because I cannot live happily alone
in this war zone
of an economic climate
because I need to be part of a solution
greater than myself
because I need to think
that we are at least
trying
to live happily ever after
together

so let's talk
you and I
let's talk
and let's figure out how
teach me how to be an ally
to your struggle

THE FUCK OFF ACCOUNT

my mum taught me how to be myself
she didn't just tell me
I could be who I wanted
or achieve what I wanted
or love who I wanted
      that was obvious

she told me, instead
to get a bank account
hers was called
'the fuck off account'
I am serious
this was the formal name
on her bank statements

she made sure she always had enough
in this account
that she would never be dependent on anyone

this is the best advice I have ever gotten
to do everything in your power
to make sure
that no employer
no partner
no organisation
no hands that feed you
are able to keep you where you do not want to be
are able to force you to do what you do not want to do
for fear of not being able to pay the rent if you leave
for fear of not being able to eat if you disagree
for fear of the future if you speak up

most people never have this privilege

but Mum had spent years building it
and she told me
no financial obstacle was going to keep her from maintaining
her integrity
so she kept a 'fuck off account'

knowing that if she ever felt she needed to up and leave
she could

just tell them to
fuck off
the rest she could figure out later

she told me
Agnes
we are lucky
we've done nothing to deserve it
but we've got it anyway
we've got rights
and we need money enough
to be unafraid to use those rights
ain't no one taking that away from us

so she told me
to get a bank account

my mum was less concerned with the identity stuff
the Barbies and the makeup
we did have women's magazines in the house
but we also had seven copies of *Das Kapital*

I didn't discover them until I already knew what it meant
to own enough of your own means of production
to never be financially dependent on the institutions you are
trying to change

she told me more simply
get a bank account
make sure you
have the financial power
to tell the idiots who think they preside over your life
the politicians
and bosses
and bureaucratic suits
the institutions and organisations
the partners (and parents)
to fuck off

and I wonder how we can talk about human rights
without talking about what makes it possible
for us to demand them
to be unafraid to use them

my mother called it
her fuck off account

on days like this
I want to make friends with the racists
– I mean
I am so tingling with happiness
I want to kiss the sexists good night
and make the homophobes
breakfast in bed

on days like this
I want to love the haters
move the head-shakers
sing the violence
lullabies

because hands
that hold on to hands
can't hold on to arms
I will hold the hands of the soldiers
interlace fingers with arms dealers
dance tango with dictators

and as I hug every person that has ever hated
let this body turn into barricades
on the battlefields
of this ignorance
let this heart become a shelter
for those made to feel without home
those made to feel they don't belong
        to anything but their own *anger*
let this mind become the round room
hate tries to find corners in
        let it try

on days like this
your hate
is turned into my hope

because talk of 'them'
should always know one of us

77

I will befriend that which wishes to call names and point fingers
wishes to tear down and destroy
wishes to build borders and create distrust

instead
if you hold hatred in your heart
I will love you
if it seeps into your actions and words
colours the lenses of your sight
blocks out the voice of
            compassion
I will love you

and I'm *ambitious* about my love

I will love you
until you love me too
until you have no choice not to
(trust me
            I can be persuasive)

I will love you until
with every thought of hatred
you can't help but know
the victims of your own intolerance
I will love you
until in every act of violence
you will feel the pain
of hurting those you love
I will love you
until to you
every repetition of this oppression
feels like an act of self-harm

I will love you until it hurts you
will hug the hatred out of you
kiss the bigotry from your lips

because love is more forgiving than hatred
I will love you
because love is more eye-opening than hatred
I will love you
because love is more transformative than hatred
I will love you

because you can't have had enough love in your childhood
if you believe in hate
I will love you

on days like this
your hate
is turned into my love for you
your clenched fist
is turned into my stretched-out hand
your closed mind
is turned into my open arms

on days like this
I can't help but invite you in
welcome
          I've been waiting for you

INDIVIDUAL HAPPINESS IS POLITICAL

Sometimes, finding the strength to be resilient is a political act.

That is why, on the many occasions when I have received death threats online because of my poetry, I consider it a political act to refuse to let this frighten me. Because choosing to be resilient in the face of structures of inequality – choosing to ask for help, to build community, to care for others – is a political act.

Often, researchers fail to account for this. Often, researchers measure happiness in numbers and on scales, removed from their contexts. Removed from resilience. Do you feel ten out of ten today?

I think that if we want to understand the ways in which happiness is always imbued with challenges and difficulty, talking about happiness as just a number is unhelpful. Rather, what if we thought of happiness as a story?

If happiness is a story, it means we have power in how we write it. It means we get to define what events are important and what characters get a leading role in the story of our lives. It means we can find strength in knowing that even if we are facing difficulties that feel overwhelming – even if right now is unbearably hard – we can still be writing a story of growth and resilience. The story we are writing about our lives can be a story of hope and heading in a promising direction. We can still be writing our way toward happy endings – not because things are perfect right now, but because we learn the most from the hardest times.

If happiness is a story, our individual stories can be intertwined with larger stories. With the stories of the people around us, and the stories of the kinds of communities and worlds we are trying to bring about. If we can connect our stories to larger stories of struggle, justice and social change, then even if right now we are living in a world that is flawed in so many ways, the story that we are writing together can be one of hopefulness, of change, and of a better tomorrow.

If happiness is a story, it gives us power in how we tell it, in how we write these stories. In how we write the story of our lives and our world. That, too, can be a political act. That, too, shapes our happiness.

I COULDN'T BE HAPPIER
Building on a quote from Shane Koyczan.

some people say
'I couldn't be happier'
like they reached the upper limit
of their joy like they aimed for the sky
reached the stars
and found the glass ceiling

some researchers say
'I couldn't be happier'
like it is possible to prove
that 50% our happiness
is determined by genetics
where do they get these numbers from?
like we shouldn't try to be any happier than we currently are
like happiness is a matter of percentage points and surveys
and it's not

I say
'I couldn't be happier'
because I don't see the point of
quantifying joy
'was I happier yesterday than I am today?'
'would I have been happier if I'd chosen that instead of this?'
'would she be happier in my place?'
happiness isn't a competition
not with yourself
and certainly not with others

I say
'I couldn't be happier'
because if I were to put my happiness
on a scale of one to ten
it would be
          something that ruins the fun of it

THIS IS MY BODY

this is my body
I thought it was time you were
formally
introduced
I mean
you've been staring at it all night
and I felt things were getting...
impolite

so I thought it time
to bring over mine
to meet yours

go ahead
take it in
this is my body
it's here for me to move in
for me to see and hear and smell and touch
it's here for me to do in

as you may have noticed
none of these functions
are for you to stare at it
or grab it as I pass you on the street
or comment on the size or shape or quality of it
as if it were up to your review

this is my body
it's here for me to dream in
for me to travel foreign seas in
it's here for me to find truth
and write poetry in
for me to climb mountains in
tear apart arguments in
watch starry skies in
fight for my life in

this is my body
it's here for me to share intimacies in
like
give a hug
and dry a tear
and hold a dying hand

for me to
dance like
we have no sorries
and tomorrow doesn't scare the shit out of us

this is my body
it's here for me to be strong in
for me to lift weights
and battle disease in
for me to run miles
and move continents in
for me to raise fists of solidarity
and punch in the face of oppression in

this is my body
it is not here for you to loudly tell me
what you would like to do with it

I came over here to clarify
this is my body
I suggest
you find your own

happy
Happy capital H
happy the women's magazine
forty-five tips for a hotter, trendier, sexier happiness
is everyone else happier than you?
we thought so
take this quiz to find out today!*

* may lead to feelings of inadequacy, stress, achievement-seeking
and general unhappiness

happy
Happy capital H
HAPPY! the new bestselling self-help book
now only £12.99 from a multinational book store near you
buy this book
to feel worse about the state of your life today

happy
Happy capital H
iHappy
McHappy
Happiness 2.0

I'd like to order a happy please
happy with a side of self-fulfilment
and a large Coke
happy with a side of personal achievement
and perfect Facebook posts
I'd like to order a happy please
happy with a side of smug

happy with a side of
better than your average life
and your dead-end job
and your snot-faced kids
and your underwhelming relationship
and your inability to
meditate
happy with a side of your dislike of meals

consisting solely of celery
happy with a side of your failures
your unaccomplishments
your dislike for getting up at 5.30 in the morning for a jog

(that's not morning
it's a great night out!)

happy as a medal
happy as a success story
happy as if happiness belonged to
Hollywood blockbusters
and advertisement companies
happiness as if it belonged to
fucking Coca-Cola

happiness as if it did not belong to you

why would we pursue a happiness
that does not belong to us?
as if our lives do not belong to us
as if the meaning of our lives is not defined by us
as if we didn't all
have to go though
the terrifying and amazing process
of figuring out what
actually
makes
us
happy

as if happiness wasn't political
as if that political choice wasn't yours
as if you could buy happiness
in a Coca-Cola can

WHEN DID YOU REALISE
or 'Questions We Have Been Asked, With One Word Changed'

When did you realise?
How did your parents take it?
How did you know, for sure, you were straight?
Did you have a lot of straight role models?
Are all your friends straight too?
And:
How can you be sure, though, if you've never had sex with
anyone of the same sex as you?
How can you be sure, though, if you've only had sex with a few
people of the same sex as you?
How can you be sure, though, if you've never had sex?

Sorry, is this making you uncomfortable?

I've heard that straight people never have sex
is that true?
I've heard that straight people have sex like all the time
is that true?
Doesn't it ever bother you that you'll be able to have kids?
Like, even if you really, really, REALLY don't want them,
you might still have kids one day?

Sorry, is this too personal?

Do you think that there was, like, a particular trauma in your
childhood that led to you being straight?
Do you believe being straight is more of a nature
or nurture thing?
Do you think that being straight is a choice?
Oh my god! I've always wanted a straight best friend! Do you
want to, like, hang out and do prescribed straight-friendly
activities together next week?

So if you're straight does that mean that you...
Like to eat food?
Occasionally listen to music?
Have hobbies?
Oh my god, me too!

So let's just get this straight, though:
if you have a partner of the opposite sex, does that mean you're straight? Or just straight-curious? Or is it like a phase thing?
If you're straight, do you, like, have to, you know, dress straight?
If you're straight, do you have to go in the Straight Parade?
How does your being straight affect your religious beliefs?
Is it true that bisexual women just make out with men to get women's attention?
Is it really hard to be both straight and white?

Sorry, is this offensive?

I can tell straight jokes, right? I mean, I have a straight friend.
I have this one totally cute straight friend, I should hook you guys up!
Did you ever watch that one TV series – you know, the one with straight people in it?
Do you know this one other straight person that I know?

Do you hate men?
Do you hate women?
Do you hate

yourself?

THIS LITTLE FIGHT OF MINE

this little fight of mine
I'm gonna let it shine
let it shine
let it shine
let it shine

when we shed light on our
struggles
our darkness
our vulnerabilities
we give others the right to do the same
and together
we make little corridors of sunshine
that let the light in

when we are unapologetically
vulnerable
scared
uncertain
overwhelmed
we give others permission
to talk about the ways in which
Everything Is Not All Right
and
I Have Nothing Figured Out
and
We're All Just Making Stuff Up As We Go Along

there is little that is as important to our wellbeing
as talking
so let's talk
not just about the easy stuff
and not just when the difficult stuff is over
but also when we're
smack down in the middle of hardship
and don't yet know our way out

when we allow ourselves to be human
in front of others
beautifully, fragilely, brokenly human
we allow others to be flawed in our presence
to raise their deepest fears
and see those fears evaporate when spoken
see their burdens lighten
when uttered

sometimes it's as easy
as singing along to the same song

this little fight of mine
I'm gonna let it shine
this little fight of mine
I'm gonna let it shine
this little fight of mine
I'm gonna let it shine
let it shine
let it shine
let it shine

THIS IS A GOOD TIME

I don't have time!
I'll do it later!
I just have to finish this project/
my degree/
raising my kids/
getting promoted at work/
living/
dying/
this season of Game of Thrones

this is just not a good time
for me

this is a great time!

to call up your dad and tell him you love him
there might not be another
ask out that girl on the bus
you may never see her again

get a dog!
you'll find a way to make it work
draw a monster on your hand
and have it tell you
all the things
        you've been afraid
                to admit to yourself
(it's a lot more fun that way)

decide to be happy

this is a good time
to cut your own hair
just to see how bad it would look
because it grows back out

this is a fantastic time
to believe in your art
to master drunken darts

to make action out of your talk
this is as good a time
as there will ever be

so ask a stranger if they'll hold you
tell your lover all those things you never do
quit your job
or get a job
or decide to work for yourself

this is a good time
to have a good time
to become who you are
to accept where you've been
to throw yourself into something new
arms   wide   open

read that book
take that trip
call up your mum
and tell her you love her

seriously
call someone
and tell them you love them
practise this every day

this is a good time
this
right here
        racing past us
                so quickly
this is a good time

what
are you
waiting
for
?

HAPPINESS IS AN ART FORM

Making art has a measurable effect on our wellbeing.

From drawing to singing in choirs to writing poetry, making art makes us happier. Art can be incredibly helpful for dealing with the difficult stuff – making art has been proven to help decrease the effects of chronic stress and ease physical pain caused by illness or disability. In other words, happiness is an art form.

It seems that when we make art – or read or watch or listen to art – our minds are for a moment completely enveloped in creativity. For a short while, we are not worrying about the past, not planning for the future. For a little while, we are completely present and without judgement of ourselves. And that makes us happier.

When we make art, it has a measurable effect on our happiness. And the beautiful thing is that it doesn't matter what kind of art we make – if we write or draw or sing or play or film or paint or animate or photograph or knit or design or program or crochet or garden. It also doesn't matter if we think that what we make is complete crap. It doesn't matter if we never show anyone what we make.

What does matter is that we create. That we express. That we write or knit or graffiti our own stories of our lives and our worlds.

When we make art about the good stuff – the things that we are grateful for in our lives and hopeful about in the world – it makes us more able to notice those things, to appreciate those things, to not take those things for granted. And that makes us happier.

When we make art about the difficult stuff – the things that we are frustrated with in our lives and angry about in the world – it makes us more able to deal with those things, to cope with those things, to change those things. And that makes us happier too.

So it doesn't matter what kind of art you make. All that matters is that for a few short moments, you create – something, anything.

And that is the art form of happiness.

you say 'poetry'
like it means pretty
wordy
flighty
girly
like it is a thing light and innocent
the flutter of a butterfly's wing
beautiful but without consequence

I say 'poetry'
like it means honesty
raw
and pulsating
still fresh from being pulled straight out of the innermost parts
of us
pungent in smell
and repulsive in its
pointing-where-you-don't-want-to-look-ness
its forcing you to take in not just the centre
but the corners
of this world
making you listen to the previously voiceless
poetry silenced for so long
            it is now screaming itself hoarse

poetry that packs a punch and a promise
to never be silent in the face of injustice
to never be without consequence

THE HEART IS A MUSCLE

I read

I read because
the heart is a muscle
and like any muscle
it needs exercise to grow stronger
we exercise
we strengthen
we grow our hearts
when we practise empathy

when we allow the thoughts and feelings of others to
permeate us
become part of us
colour the way we see the world

we practise empathy
when we read about others' experiences
others' challenges and victories
others' lived worlds and fictional realities
when we allow others' truths
to be equal to our own
as real as our own
as important as our own

reading is growing our horizons
strengthening our invisible bonds to others
linking our stories with theirs
letting empathy shape and sharpen
our solidarity
our outlook
our way of being in the world

I read because the heart is a muscle
and like any muscle
it needs exercise
empathy is that exercise
reading is how we grow our hearts

I write

I write because the heart is a muscle
and like any muscle
it needs stretching
making art is how we stretch our hearts

telling our stories
sharing our truths
is how we release the tension
of pent-up stress
undo the pressure from constant use
of the heart
we create art
to make an outlet for all the steam
made in the pressure cooker of our insides
it makes it bearable
to live in a world so full of suffering
both our own and others'
it lets a little space in
to notice the sunshine too

I write because it makes me human
because it allows me
to talk to myself
honestly
because it lets me speak to people I have never met
and may never come to meet
because it lets me speak to you

I write because art transcends me
survives me
is bigger than me
because my story is connected with others
our joys
our challenges
are intertwined
yours and mine
part of the same patchwork
the same epic poem
of humanity

I write because the brain
can be trained
to reshape and reform itself
because we can sketch new neural pathways
new patterns of practice
when we write our way there

I write because the heart is a muscle
and like any muscle
it needs stretching
making art is how we stretch our hearts

I read and write because it
literally
physically
changes who I am
on a synapse level
makes me more of what I want to be
less of what I am afraid to become

I make art
because the heart is a muscle
and it must be trained

WRITING HAPPINESS

There are studies that show that reading, watching, listening to arts makes us happier. But those studies also show that making our own art makes us even more happy. Adds even more to our ability to build resilience. To celebrate the good. To appreciate the whole of life's rollercoaster ride, getting us through rock bottom and helping us cherish the view from the peaks.

So I thought it was time I gave you some practical exercises for boosting your own wellbeing – through creative writing.

This book has existed in many shapes and forms. At first, it was an idea. An idea that led me to deciding to live according to happiness research. To write about the good and the bad. And to think about what it would mean to take happiness seriously – personally, socially, politically.

Then this book was a TED talk. It was called 'What I've Learned From Studying Happiness' and it was a chance to combine the science with the art. From that TED talk, this book became a one-woman spoken word show. It was called If You're Happy and You Know It – Take This Survey and it toured festivals for science, wellbeing and arts, winning awards and praise as it went along.

In the process of becoming a book, this book also became a workshop series. It was called the Wellbeing Writing Workshops, and it involved putting all the most important lessons I had learned from the science of happiness into practice. Into practical creative writing exercises for some wonderful people who were struggling.

This last section of the poetry collection is made up of writing exercises from that workshop series. Some of the exercises come from scientific studies. Some from arts therapies. Some from meditation techniques. Some, I quite simply made up.

So here we are, at the end and at the beginning. This is the point when I stop writing and you start. When I stop talking and you begin to tell your own story. The following exercises are some ways to get started. To create your own art form. To build your own happiness.

I think it's time you begun.

Note: I have left some pages after each writing exercise for you to fill yourself. Feel free to use them to write your own happiness. To try and fail and try again. To build resilience. To remember the good. To reflect on your life, your good times and your bad.

There are more blank pages at the end of the book as well. Feel free to use them!

WRITING EXERCISES

MIND BLOB: A WRITING EXERCISE

For building coping mechanisms

NEED:

paper
a pen
a timer (a phone will do, but set it to flight mode to
avoid distractions)

1) Set the timer to four minutes.

2) From when the timer starts to when it stops, don't stop
writing. Write any and everything that is on your mind. Write it
in whatever form it comes out.

If you find yourself unable to think of anything, just write 'I don't
know what to write' over and over until you find something.

If you find your mind and pen are heading toward a difficult part
of your experiences where you don't want to go right now, just
write 'I don't know what to write' until you find something else.

3) When the timer goes off, stop writing.

4) Now, without a time constraint, write down three emotions
you are feeling right now. They can be abstract like 'empty' or
'overwhelmed' or concrete like 'happy' or 'angry'.

5) Write down three physical sensations you can feel on or
inside your body right now. Abstract like 'achy' and concrete
like 'hungry' are both fine.

When you've finished, put down your pen. You did it.

Whatever you wrote down is more than good enough.

Whatever came up, as soon as you put down the pen you can
choose to leave it behind, on the page. Or you can choose to
think about it some more. That is up to you.

This writing exercise is based on a meditation technique of grounding yourself in your body.

It is a way of checking in on yourself, to take better care of yourself. It is a way to look for warning signs if you are not feeling too well and need a little extra support from yourself or others. It is a way to celebrate and remember how good you are feeling when you feel good. It is a way of being in touch with what's going on with you, rather than bottling it up.

If you find this exercise helpful, make an effort to do it often. Taking a few minutes every morning to do this exercise can be a great way to better support yourself through the day by checking in on yourself.

If the exercise wasn't helpful to you – don't worry. Not everything works the same for everyone. Try a different writing exercise instead.

MIND BLOB

REMEMBERING THE GOOD STUFF: A WRITING EXERCISE

For building resilience

NEED:

paper
a pen
a timer (a phone will do, but set it to flight mode to avoid distractions)

This writing exercise is similar to the Patronus Charm in the Harry Potter books and comes from an age-old meditation technique. The idea is this: really good memories can help us battle demons, whether internal or external.

This is how to do it.

1) First, pick a memory. A really good memory. It can be a memory of a time when you did something really nice for someone, or someone did something really nice for you, a time you achieved something you're proud of, or just a moment when you felt really good.

Got it? Good.

Try to remember that memory as vividly as possible.

2) Write down three things you could see at the time of the memory. If you don't remember exactly, let your imagination take over – what might you have seen?

Try not to second-guess yourself.

3) Now write down three things you could hear at the time of the memory. Silence? Birdsong? Music? Anything is fine.

4) Write down three things you could smell. The ocean? Food cooking? Anything is fine.

5) Write down three things you could taste. Toothpaste? Saltwater? Whatever comes to mind, write it down.

6) Finally, write down three things you could feel on your skin or in your body at the time. Your heartbeat? Grass under your feet? Someone holding your hand?

However many words you managed to write down is fine.

7) Looking at all the words you've written down, circle three to five words. You don't have to pick them for any particular reason – maybe they look nice on the page, maybe they most vividly describe the memory. Just circle a few.

8) You now have your base for writing a story about your memory. Put the timer on five minutes, and write about your memory. Try to use all the words you circled.

From when the timer starts to when it stops, keep writing. Don't worry about how it turns out. The point is remembering. The point is writing your own story.

9) When the timer goes off – stop writing.

You have just produced your very own Patronus Charm. A vivid memory to return to when things are tough, to help you remember there are times when things are not as hard. And there will be times like that again. This, too, shall pass.

REMEMBERING THE GOOD STUFF

REMEMBERING THE GOOD STUFF

RECIPE FOR SELF-CARE: A WRITING EXERCISE

For self-care

NEED:

paper
a pen
a timer (a phone will do, but set it to flight mode to avoid distractions)

Try not to judge what you write.
Try not to second-guess what you write.
Try not to over-think spelling or grammar.
Try not to worry about if it's any good.
That's not the point.

The point is the writing.

No matter what comes out when you write or what you think of it, the point is the writing.

1) Simply set the timer to four minutes and start.

2) Write a recipe for self-care.

What ingredients will you need?
What instructions would you give for mixing them?
Do you have any tips for the person baking self-care, any tips for yourself?

Go ahead and start.

3) Between when timer starts and timer rings, keep writing.

Don't stop for anything (unless your hand cramps up).

If you run out of things to write, write 'I don't know what to write' on repeat – until you find something else to write.

4) When the timer goes off – stop.

5) Repeat until you stop judging yourself and your writing.

Repeat until you are able to follow your own instructions for self-care.

RECIPE FOR SELF-CARE

RECIPE FOR SELF-CARE

WHAT IS IN OUR POWER: A WRITING EXERCISE

For building coping mechanisms

NEED:

paper
a pen
a timer (a phone will do, but set it to flight mode to avoid distractions)

1) Set timer to three minutes.

2) Alternate between sentences starting with 'it is in my power to...' and sentences starting with 'it is not in my power to...'.

Finish the sentence with whatever comes to mind.

Try not to second-guess yourself.
Try not to judge what you are writing.
Any and everything that comes out is fine.

3) When the timer goes off, stop writing.

This is a way to remember what you can do to support yourself, and what is completely unreasonable to expect of yourself.

As people who experience stress and mental ill-health, we often tend to blame ourselves for not feeling better, not doing better, not being enough somehow. It is incredibly important to remember that it is not your fault that you are struggling. Some things are in our power, and some things are not. Let us focus on what we can do, rather than what we can't.

Try not to blame yourself for what it is not in your power to do or affect. You are not to blame for struggling. You are strong for continuing on. Try to remember that.

WHAT IS IN OUR POWER

WHAT IS IN OUR POWER

For celebrating the good

NEED:

a newspaper
a black marker pen
a timer (a phone will do, but set it to flight mode to avoid distractions)

Often we are told certain stories about what we are and who we are, what we are and are not capable of, how much we have succeeded or failed. But we have the power to rewrite those stories, to shape our own narratives of the struggles and victories of our lives.

This exercise is a way to put that idea into practice, on a smaller (and more arts and crafts-y) scale.

1) Take a page from an old newspaper. It doesn't matter what the story on the page is. Try not to read it or pay too much attention to it.

2) Set the timer to six minutes.

3) Grab your black marker pen and start at the top of the page. Use the marker pen to black out all the words you don't need. The words you leave unmarked by the marker pen should form a new story.

This new story doesn't have to make sense. It doesn't have to be grammatically correct. But it will be something brand-new. It will be a story you made with the (newspaper) story you were handed.

This is a fun arts and crafts writing exercise, as well as a good metaphor for this lesson: you shape your own story. You are not a failure. You are not weak. You are not what anyone else defines you as. You are a fighter, and only you know what you have had to fight.

You matter.

LETTER TO A STRANGER: A WRITING EXERCISE

For building empathy and compassion

NEED:

a newspaper
scissors
paper
a pen
a timer (a phone will do, but set it to flight mode to avoid distractions)

1) Open the newspaper. Find a picture of someone you don't know and don't know of. Cut out the picture without reading the story about them.

2) Put the timer on four minutes.

3) Write a letter entitled 'Dear Stranger' to the person in the picture.

Start your letter with 'Dear stranger, I want you to know' and keep writing until the timer goes off. Try to imagine what their joys are, what their challenges are, what kind of support or advice you could offer them. What they might be able to teach you. Ask questions, or answer them. Imagine that you could actually send the letter to them.

4) When the timer goes off, stop.

See what happens. What you think. How your compassion for a total stranger might also make you better at being compassionate to the people in your life – and to yourself.

LETTER TO A STRANGER

LETTER TO A STRANGER

TIMELINE OF LEARNING: A WRITING EXERCISE

For celebrating the good

NEED:

 paper
a pen

1) Starting with age 1, and working yourself to your current age, write down one thing you have learnt each year since you were born. Whatever you think of first is fine.

In other words:
'Age 1: learnt to walk'
and
'Age 13: learnt that I love sci-fi books'
are both forms of learning.

Learning to walk or talk or read or write are all pretty big deals. If you are able to take those things for granted, you are lucky. Celebrate them. But it is also a big deal to learn about yourself, about who you are and what you like. And so is learning about the people around you, the world around you, about new skills and places you didn't know before. If you are able to do those things, try to appreciate that ability. Celebrate your timeline of learning.

This is a way to change your thinking, to stop seeing each challenge as a make-or-break moment, as success or failure – and to begin to see each thing we learn now as the most recent point in a long timeline of learning.

Learning is accumulative. We learn from our mistakes and our achievements, our failures and our successes. Each new thing we learn builds on what we have learnt before. Because each new challenge does not define you. Each new challenge does not undo all the learning you have done before. It just adds to the large and growing pile of things you are capable of. It is just the most recent point in your lifelong timeline of learning.

TIMELINE OF LEARNING

QUESTIONS AND ANSWERS: A WRITING EXERCISE

For building empathy and compassion (drawing on the poem 'Questions and Answers, In No Particular Order' by Sarah Kay)

NEED:

 paper
a pen

First, write down your answers to these questions, each on a new line:

What has been your favourite thing this week?

What is your favourite food?

What is the first thing you hear when you wake up in the morning?

How long have you been trying to self-care?

What do you hope for for the future?

Where would you be right now if you could be anywhere?

Now you've got your answers. It's time to write down some of your own questions. Write down:

A question you have been asked in the last 24 hours

A question you wish you had the answer to

A question you often ask

A question you wish you had been asked

A question you maybe, possibly, perhaps know the answer to

A question you definitely know the answer to

You've got your questions and your answers. Using only these, match them up and see if one can in some small way answer the other.

Because you have the answers you are looking for, if only you trust them.

For self-care

paper
a pen
a timer (a phone will do, but set it to flight mode to avoid distractions)

1) First, imagine yourself as you are on difficult days, or when things feel unimaginably hard.

Then write down three thoughts you tend to think when you feel like that.

Try not to over-think or judge what you are writing.

2) Next, write down three emotions you tend to feel when you are having a hard time. These can be abstract like 'empty' or concrete like 'angry'. Anything is fine.

3) Finally, write down three physical sensations you tend to experience when you are having a hard time. Anything you can feel on your skin or in your body counts. Headaches or chest pain or an itchy toe? Write it down.

4) Now look at the paper in front of you and imagine a good friend of yours told you this was how they were thinking and feeling. What would you want to tell them?

5) Set timer for four minutes.

6) Write a letter to the friend who is feeling the way you feel when you feel bad. What would you want them to know? Remember? Do? What advice would you give?

7) When the timer goes off, stop writing. You did it.

If it is not properly finished – don't worry.

If it didn't turn out the way you'd planned – don't worry.

You wrote something. And that counts.

In fact, it very likely added to your long-term wellbeing. So keep writing. Keep making art. Even if you think it's crap. Even if you don't want to show it to anyone.

Because every piece of research indicates that this will see you through difficulty and help you enjoy the good stuff more.

So just make art, OK?

LETTER TO A FRIEND

LETTER TO A FRIEND

WRITING ON

If you've enjoyed writing and want to try some more of this, I run an online writing circle and backstage blog about new projects and events.

You can go onto www.patreon.com/AgnesTorokPoet and become a Patron (a supporter of my art). Once you're a Patron, you can make more art with me in the writing circle, get a say in what I should make more art about, and see anything new I release 24 hours before it goes public.

The Patreon site is also a great channel to send me what you wrote in your writing exercises (if you'd like!), or to just chat with me about art and happiness.

You can also find me on social media (fb, twitter, Youtube) and tell me what you thought of the book.

I would love to hear from you!

Agnes

HAPPINESS MANIFESTO

Before I leave you to write your own story, to craft your own happiness, to reflect on your own joys and challenges – through poetry, short stories and arts and crafts – I wanted to say thank you.

Thank you for reading. Thank you for listening. Thank you for taking this time.

Writing this book has meant an awful lot to me. And I am so glad that you are reading it right now. You're definitely adding to my happiness! Thank you for that.

And finally, I wanted to leave you with one last poem. It's my manifesto for making art. And the reason I think you should join that choir / take that crochet class / get that instrument / try these writing exercises / just make some art – if you haven't already.

Here it is – one last poem from me (for now).

ART FOR ART'S SAKE

I've never been much for art for art's sake
if it doesn't do anything for us
why do we spend so much time doing it?

I want poetry like first touch
poetry that kisses me so deeply
metaphors linger on my tongue

I want poetry that claws at my heartstrings
opens my chest and lets itself in
I want poetry
that fucks me senseless
poetry that gives me morning-after hair

the day after a really good poem
I like to walk home in the morning light
still dressed from last night
shoes in hand
smiling uncontrollably
just thinking about the best bits of last night's
poem

I've never been much for art for art's sake
if it doesn't do anything to us
why do we spend so much time doing it?
I want poetry to be the soundtrack to my life
poetry to plug my headphones into
poems to laugh and dance to
cry and meditate to

I want poems strong enough and versatile enough
to listen to on repeat
like a heartbeat

I've never been much for art for art's sake
if it doesn't change any part of us
why do we spend so much time changing it?
I need poems
poems like rescue boats

and electric blankets
poems to calm my mind
and kick-start my heart

most of all
most of all I need poems like anthems
poems like manifestos and marches
poems that are both our weapons
and our shields
poems that build an
us
that can keep fighting
to ask real questions
and demand real responsibility
poems that build a real community
of us
worth fighting for

I've never been much for art for art's sake
I want poems
that change my life
and rock my world
and I want
you

to write them

I want to say a huge thank you to the people who have made this possible.

Firstly, to my big and wonderful family who have supported me every step of the way. I would not be who I am today without each and every one of you. To all my parents. All my siblings. My cousins and aunts and uncles and grandparents. To the whole of the extended inosculation – thank you.

Special thank you to Emily Still, poetry wife and companion in all matters poetical, who looked at a first draft of this collection and (reassuringly) told me it wasn't all shite. Thank you for getting me through the difficult bits.

To those in the poetry community in Sweden, Scotland, the rest of the UK and across the world who have been supportive, who have given me chances to learn, to perform, and to develop. Who have backed me up when I most needed it. Thank you.

Thank you to all the wonderful crowdfunding supporters who have helped me live off what I love. For your enthusiasm and your support – thank you.

Thank you to those who booked, went to see, and supported the *If You're Happy and You Know It – Take This Survey* show. Thank you to good friends who didn't complain when I endlessly rehearsed – and forced them to listen.

Thank you to Edinburgh University Students' Association for funding me in turning the show into a workshop series. Thank you to all the Wellbeing Writers who made all that work worth it. For sharing, and writing, and helping create the Wellbeing Writing Collection. You are all wonderful.

Finally, a huge thank you to Clive Birnie, Harriet Evans and Burning Eye Books for making this book happen.

I still can't actually believe that it has. Look at that, twelve-year-old me (with dreams of being a published poet) – WE DID IT!

EXTRA PAGES FOR EXERCISES

EXTRA PAGES FOR EXERCISES

EXTRA PAGES FOR EXERCISES

EXTRA PAGES FOR EXERCISES

EXTRA PAGES FOR EXERCISES

EXTRA PAGES FOR EXERCISES

EXTRA PAGES FOR EXERCISES

EXTRA PAGES FOR EXERCISES

EXTRA PAGES FOR EXERCISES

Thank you for reading.
With love and solidarity,
Agnes

Lightning Source UK Ltd.
Milton Keynes UK
UKOW07f0635011116
286606UK00014B/56/P